Feel Great Now

How to Dissolve Stress, Think Clearly, Eliminate Headaches and Sleep Through the Night.

Hale Brownlee & Janá Parker

Feel Great Now

2nd Edition

ISBN 978-1500416393

Printed in USA

Dedication

This book is dedicated to my sons Matthew & Benjamin whom I (Hale) love dearly and to my parents who believed in me and supported me through difficult times.

In addition I would like to dedicate this book to all seekers of truth. May it aide you in your journey and provide tangible improvements to the quality of your life.

\- Hale Brownlee

Damon, may this aid you in your journey.

Throughout this book one of the authors may relate a situation or tell a story. When this happens the authors name will be placed in parenthesis after the first reference to the author.

Feel Great Now

Acknowledgements

It is with the deepest gratitude that I (Hale) wish to thank all those in the scientific and spiritual communities from whom I learned so much as they were the catalyst for my transformation into the person I am today.

First, I want to thank the movie "What The Bleep Do We Know" for awakening my natural scientific curiosity. Ironically, it was taking a hard look at the works of scientists including Robert G Jahn, Brenda J Dunne, Roger D. Nelson, Dean Radin, Cleve Backster and Dale Pond which shattered my fixed and limiting engineering mentality and opened my eyes to previously unimaginable possibilities.

Armed with the viewpoint that spirituality and science are simply two different languages speaking to the mysteries of the universe, I set out to study both the outer workings of universe and the inner workings of my mind.

On my quest for inner spiritual truth and awakening, I wish to thank the following teachers in the order that I encountered them:

- Barbara and Robert Klein who taught me aikido, a martial art that is moving meditation.

- Dale Sims and Madonna Machado who gave me Avatar training.

- The Dali Lama for being a living example of what one person can do and be in the world as well as his lightness and sense of humor even in the face of the difficult issues facing humanity.

- DavidPaul & Candace Doyle for teaching me to hear the voice for love within me.

- Dr. David Hawkins for applying the scientific method to spirituality and for his book Power Vs. Force which opened my mind to many new ideas.

- David Morelli who trained me to use my intuition and to read energy and all my friends from the Enwaken program who helped me clear my subconscious blocks.

- Burt Goldman for his Quantum Jumping program which taught me how to use my imagination to have experiences and bring in knowledge from alternate realities.

- Esther & Jerry Hicks for the awareness of the positive changes that channeling can create in peoples' lives and for helping me understand the need for it. And also for their book, "Ask & it is given", which inspired the idea for this book.

- Fred Van Liew who taught me energy healing modalities.

- Kristin Abbajay and the staff at Denver Landmark Education for teaching me the importance of un-creating instead of building on top of my existing mess.

- Gabrielle Spencer for helping me clear blocks on many levels and contributing to my spiritual growth and education.

- Janá Parker for being a conduit through which the mid-consciousness techniques emerged as well as co-authoring this book with me.

- Coral Thomas for encouraging me, believing in me and giving me the occasional kick in the hindquarters when needed.

- The Secret To Life Coaching for providing a space for me to evolve and share my wisdom and to my friends and fellow coaches who helped me become all that I am.

- Paul Caire who filled in many gaps in my training and helped me deepen my connection and understanding.

- John Morton for telling me, "You can do it all".

- John Roger for creating the Movement of Spiritual Inner Awareness. I love how "For the highest good of all concerned" has woven itself into my life and this book.

- Doug Krueger for the introduction to Higher Brain Living

- Ron and Mary Hulnick for inspiration and an excellent couples workshop.

Finally, I would like to thank Susan Morrison for helping me grow personally, spiritually and in my experiential understanding of conscious partnership. Your support, help and encouragement while I was writing this book means everything to me. This book is much better because of your feedback, editing and contributions. The way you hold for excellence, authenticity, truth and greatness deeply inspires me and challenges me to be the best I can be. Behind every good man is a great woman. Thanks for being my great woman! I love you.

I did not name everyone who contributed to my awakening and the subsequent unfolding of this book. However, I want you to know that even if you were not named, you are valued and loved and I deeply appreciate your contribution.

Love & Light,

Hale Brownlee

Feel Great Now

I (Janá) stand in gratitude. It is a natural and pleasant state of mind. It is effortless and fun for there is a huge world of beauty for which to be grateful. As I continue to practice Mid-Consciences it lifts me from one level of excitement to the next higher level. I find that I love moments of solitude so that I wave my magic wand and send myself to different places never dreamed of before.

In gratitude I wish to thank my I-friends. To all the inter-dimensionals that helped us so much I say thanks. For me it was Artemus, OB and Sparky. For Hale it was Weus group. They are so wonderful and amazing to be with. I so much enjoy channeling.

There are those in my 3-D life that are so important. Thank you Ibrahim for standing in the space to support me in all that I do. Thank you for allowing our lives to continue in the luxury that you have provided. It is so beautiful in our paradise. Thank you Miranda, my awesome daughter, for being the strong, independent, individual who continues to astonish and bless us with your many successes. My life overflows with so many amazing friends that support and encourage me on a regular base.

Janá Parker

Table of Contents

Preface

It has been such a great honor to channel this information for Hale Brownlee. I (Janá) have learned so much through the process of making the book. It is also very amazing what I have learned about myself. In the very first few channels Hale did ask a lot of questions. I was almost afraid they might leave but it seemed to bond the relationship and define the purpose. One thing that is so amazing to me is why Hale did not begin to channel. What they said was that he has, and has always had, knowing. This knowing is a much higher form of connecting to Higher Consciousness than just repeating what words there are in a message. So I say thanks Hale as you have endured the test of time and unwrapped the meaning and then brought it down to us. Now we can access this information in a step by step process. Now we can make sense of making our brains function at a more masterful level.

I want you to know in the beginning that this program was very hard for me to do. But it has grown me more than any other single training I have ever done. My mind has transformed from the "I should've, would've, could've" looping insanity to I AM. For those that live in this mind trap be patient and loving with yourself. Find the profound beauty of experiencing life in an altered state: Divine Bliss.

Light and Love,

Janá Parker

After holding my first live event where I (Hale) taught the participants how to tune into their intuition and to read energy, a longing to teach something that was uniquely my own began to bubble up inside me. I set the intention for this to happen and forgot about it. While I went about the next few months, the universe brought together situations and circumstances that allowed my desire to be realized. In new age vernacular I would say, "My intention manifested in this volume of work." From a Christian point of view I would say, "My prayers were answered." The perspective I choose to see it through does not affect what happened, only how I make sense of it.

My Christian upbringing taught me that God uses everything around us to communicate with us. Whether it is a phrase from the pastor's sermon that impacted me or a bumper sticker on the car in front of me, that seemed strangely relevant to the questions I was asking, it is all God communicating with me. In addition, I learned that God has beings that serve him such as the Angels that watch over us. I was also taught to fear the occult; that there were dark forces in the universe that I should be wary of.

As my spiritual education continued, my Christian beliefs were broadened to include teachings from other religions such as Buddhism and New Age philosophies. Loving is the core viewpoint of all the teachings I encountered and therefore I found them compatible and integrated them into my belief system.

On July 11, 2012 I went to La Junta, Colorado to learn how to channel. Channeling is a way to allow God, Angels or other non-physical beings to communicate with you. It is a tool just like a phone that can be used for good or evil depending on who you are talking to and what your intention is.

As I worked with Janá Parker, it became apparent that leaning to channel was not in my highest good, as the ways I currently receive communication from God were better suited for me. I was a little disappointed as I wanted to hear words, as many of my friends did, and receive guidance that way but I was also thankful for the way I receive information as inner knowing or intuition.

The next morning Janá told me that there were five different groups that wanted to talk to me and I could talk to any, all or none of them. I asked Janá to have each group give me a summary of what they were about. After listening to the five summaries, I had two of the groups to give me more details and then chose the group that offered the information on Mid-Consciousness, which is described in this book.

Mid-Consciousness is higher dimensional wisdom that I agreed to bring into this world. When I asked about it I received the following story:

> *Before I took physical form in this 3rd dimensional world, I made an agreement to bring forth this information. This contract was between myself, God and twelve other beings, some of which are in physical form today and some that are not. As I took form here and grew up in this world, I lost touch with this information. Throughout my life there have been many situations and circumstances that pointed me in the direction of awakening and remembering. Most of them I blatantly ignored. However, the longing to teach my own work persisted*

4

*because it stemmed from the contract I
made to bring forward this teaching.*

To my engineering side, this story seems bizarre but when I feel into it, the story feels true. Regardless of whether I believe the story or not the techniques in this book have helped people just like you reduce stress and feel more alive. That is proof enough for me. It still amazes me that reducing stress can get rid of headaches, help you sleep better and even improve or eliminate chronic pain. However, one thing I have learned on my journey is to never underestimate the power of my mind.

This book is the first of a series of three books which teach humans to live in higher consciousness as they go about their daily lives. It has been a delightful journey bringing forth this wisdom. To this day, the way in which I accessed this information seems strange to me. If it is mine, why couldn't I access it directly? What I now get, when I ask myself this question is:

*When you began this journey with us, if
we had expressed ourselves as a part of
you, you would not have valued the
information, as at that time you did not
value yourself and did not feel like you
had anything great to contribute to the*

> *world.* *Because* *this* *information*
> *appeared to come from a source greater*
> *than you, you acted on it and created*
> *transformational workshops and this*
> *book thus fulfilling your agreement*
> *sooner rather than later.*

During the early stages of this book, when I asked the Mid-Consciousness group to identify themselves, they replied through Janá, "We are the higher consciousness of Hale Brownlee." For some reason, that was not enough for me. I wanted them to have a cool name and be something bigger and greater as I did not truly value who I was.

When I pressed them for a name they gave me "WEUS" which is WE + US. It is written as the proper name "Weus" which is pronounced woose (like goose but with a "w" instead of a "g"). The "WE" are the 12 original participants and the "US" are those of us, both physical and non-physical who aide, support or participate in Mid-Consciousness. So when I say "Join US" it is a genuine invitation to belong to this group.

The Weus group is loving, gentle, humble, light and even funny at times though often their jokes get lost in translation. For example when asked if they wanted to be credited in the book, they answered:

"It does not matter to us: we won't make a dime off it either way."

This is quite funny if you think about how little use non-physical beings would actually have for a dime. To conclude this section I will share what Weus said when asked about their purpose:

"Weus now shows you Oneness as our goal. Weus uses Mid-Consciousness to increase mind power so that you can hold the Higher-Consciousness thoughts. As you develop this in your minds it is easier to understand all things. We see that many minds are ready for this goal and will invest in the time to make it happen."

Light & Love,

Hale Brownlee

Introduction

Have you ever been watching TV and something comes on that you don't like? Well what do you do? You don't sit there and go, "This is an awful program. I'm so sick of it I wish they wouldn't play this stuff all the time!" No, you pick up your remote control, you click a button and you change it. It's that simple.

Why is it that when you are going through your day and something happens that you don't like and you are experiencing anger or frustration, that you get stuck in the feeling? What if you could just click a button in your mind and change it? What if it is that easy?

You may say "I can't just leave when my boss is chewing me out." This is true and you are referring to the outer experience. We will all experience situations in the world that are unpleasant or even down right rotten. Changing the channel is not running away or avoiding your responsibilities. It is simply choosing to have a different experience.

You may ask:

> *"Is it really possible to change*
> *how I am feeling when I'm in a*

9

> *challenging situation such as my*
> *boss yelling at me?"*

Absolutely!   People just like you have used the techniques in this book to shift their state and have a pleasant experience despite their outer circumstances. You may be wondering:

"What other types of situations is it good for?"

How about dealing with traffic as illustrated in the following story:

I (Hale) got up extra early one Saturday morning, loaded up my skis and headed out on the two hour drive to Cooper Mountain. I was planning to be one of the first to play in the fresh powder but about half way there the traffic on I-70 slowed to about 10 miles per hour. My plans of arriving before the lift opened were shattered and I became incredibly frustrated at being stuck in traffic. There was nothing I could do, no alternate route to take. If I wanted to ski that day, I had to sit in traffic. So I decided to play a different game. Instead of being frustrated at all the traffic, I imagined that each car was a fish swimming in the ocean with me. The blue ones were dolphins, the trucks were whales and so on. After a few minutes I was actually having fun "swimming" in all the traffic. My trip to the slopes took three hours instead of two, yet I thoroughly enjoyed the trip and arrived in great spirits more relaxed and grateful for the day than normal.

You see it's not what is happening to you that matters; it's how you relate to your experience. Let's swing it the other way.

> *Have you ever been on vacation at the beach, it's a beautiful sunny day, just the perfect temperature, with a gentle breeze and instead of feeling relaxed and joyful, you are angry about something that happened last week?*

If so then it must be obvious that it's not what is happening in the moment that has control of how you are feeling.

This is great news because you can't always control what happens to you. While you can make smart choices, if you choose to live it, your life will still be full of heartbreaks, misunderstandings and those ironic moments like "rain on your wedding day". Of course you can choose to play it safe, not get involved, play a small game and not fully participate so you don't get hurt. Unfortunately, in my experience, this leads to life becoming dull, boring and

11

depressing, which often creates the hurt I (Hale) was seeking to avoid. You may be wondering:

> *"If what is happening in the moment does not control how I am feeling then what does?"*

If you ponder this for a moment you may arrive at the correct answer: You do! You are 100% in control of how you experience each moment. Believe me this is exciting news because if you are in control you can change it.

However, you may not believe you are in control of how you experience each moment because it has not been your experience in the past. Your mood has always been swung by the events that happened to you, are happening to you or might happen to you. This is normal. Like a baby, who has not yet learned to walk, most of us have not learned how to direct our mind. We are therefore limited to crawling around in the emotional muck our external experiences create. Once your mind can stand tall and survey your emotional landscape, you can then choose how you want to feel.

About ten years ago I (Hale) was just like you. Despite being a successful software architect, earning a six figure income and moving his family to Hawaii, I was frequently frustrated, angry or depressed. I spent a lot of time stressed out about things that might happen and life had become dull. Apparently achieving everything I had dreamed of; living on a five acre estate in paradise, working from home, having a great wife and family, being my own boss and making lots of money was not the answer.

> ## *"If being "successful" is not the answer then'what is?"*

This question haunted me until one day I became fed up and started looking for solutions. My ten year journey took me through many highs and lows and has culminated in the creation of the system described in this book that allows virtually anyone to take charge of their mind and change their mood so they can have more happiness, peace, joy or relaxation whenever they desire. Your mind is amazingly powerful and you are invited to learn how to direct it so that you can create more of what you want to experience in your life instead of letting it roam freely and taking what it throws at you.

- Imagine you could buy five minutes of, peace, joy, awe, bliss or whatever feeling you desired. How much would that be worth to you?

- How much money and how much time would you invest?

- Do your kids, or spouse know that one thing that sends you through the roof?

- If it were possible, how much would you be willing to pay a brain surgeon to reprogram your brain so that you can behave differently when your buttons are pushed?

By reading this book and doing the exercises you will learn how to:

- Create an experience of peace, joy, awe, bliss or whatever feeling you desire.

- Reprogram your triggers so that you can respond differently instead of reacting the way you always do.

- Feel more peaceful and relaxed.

- Experience the euphoric state we call Divine Bliss.

- Experience higher states of consciousness.

- Change how you are feeling (for example from sad to joyful).

- Use movement to intensify your experience so that you can feel amazing while interacting in the world.

- When a situation triggers you, you can put a stop to it by reprogramming the trigger.

The goal of this book is not only to educate you on what is possible, but to provide a simple system that allows you to create the results listed above or something even better in your life.

Chapter One
Understanding Mid-Consciousness

After reading this book you will have powerful tools that allow you to shift into your intended state at will and to create new pathways in your brain. If you want more information on the benefits of using the techniques described in this book please read the IntroductionIntroductionIntroductionIntroductionIntroductionIntroduction, p. 9.

The core techniques taught in this book allow you to access a state of awareness called Mid-Consciousness. That name was chosen because it initially appeared to be a space in between the conscious and subconscious mind, something that was neither conscious nor subconscious, but containing properties of both. Instead, Mid-Consciousness now appears to be an access point to the entire mind including both the conscious and subconscious. It is defined as follows:

Mid-Consciousness is a state of awareness where the conscious and subconscious mind are acting in harmony.

In this state it is possible to virtually reprogram the brain in ways that will potentially enhance your life. For example, you can recall information from your subconscious mind and bring it back to your conscious mind. You can also consciously adjust your subconscious programming. For example, you can reprogram yourself to respond differently to a situation or circumstance that triggers you.

Permission to learn what you need

When we teach workshops they often start with giving you permission to use what is beneficial to you:

> *You have permission to retain all information as given. You have permission to use the parts that you need and discard the rest. You have permission to be in a relaxed state of consciousness so that your subconscious can work and understand the material presented in this book.*

We invite you to read the permission statement above aloud substituting "I" for "You". This will prepare your mind to absorb the information in this book.

A Dialogue with Mid-Consciousness

The best way to introduce you to Mid-Consciousness is through the dialogue below as this is how we were introduced to it.

Mid-C: Hello Reader. This is Mid-Consciousness. I am the place in your mind that is ready and waiting to be at Higher Consciousness.

Reader: I have tried all that and I just don't have the time to spend "getting there".

Mid-C: That is why Higher Consciousness can now be integrated into your normal daily life. It can now be accessed using a single symbol and can be done any time during your day and at any activity level.

Reader: I have enough trouble keeping my mind focused on what I'm doing without having to think about something else.

Mid-C: Yes, I know that you spend most of your day in non-productive repetitions, thought patterns that are negative, judgmental and harmful to your mind, body and soul.

Reader: I can't control my thoughts that's why I … (do some kind of habitual, addictive or destructive behavior).

Mid-C: I can help you grow your mind so that it is big enough to replace all that with love, willingness and peace.

19

So now we begin the journey to unlock the hidden potential in your mind so that you can choose how you experience your life. We tell you now that this is not only possible, but that people just like you have already done it.

Terminology

We will now address the mind and provide it with a context to understand this teaching by creating a shared vocabulary.

If you have read self-help or new age literature, you probably heard the terms "conscious" and "subconscious" but what do they really mean? Even the word "consciousness" has an array of different interpretations and meanings. Since we have to start somewhere, let's start with a definition:

> *Mid-Consciousness is a state of awareness where the conscious and subconscious mind are acting in harmony.*

Before we can further explain Mid-Consciousness we must first agree on the meanings of words used to define it. Since this book is intended for a broad audience and our usage of certain terms may be different than the mainstream interpretation, we will start by defining the words in question.

Filters are an individual's perspective, based on past experiences that have them believe in or interpret their world in a certain way. They are created from past experiences based on the individual's truth about all that they experienced before. A filter can be thought of as a lens which brings certain things into sharp focus while blurring other aspects or a pair of glasses which adds tint or color to every experience.

Consciousness Mind is your mind with your filters running. Everything is filtered through your perspective: what you think your loved one will want, or your value system. All of these cloud your reality by skewing the what you perceive. When two people observe the same event and have different experiences of what happened it is because each person's conscious mind observed the event through its filters.

Subconscious Mind is your mind without filters. It collects only facts without any filters of personal interest. It records the actual circumstance without interference. It is exactly what the film will say every time it is played.

Awareness is using your six senses to understand your present set of circumstances. The sixth sense is your intuition or inner guidance. When you are fully aware, you are not just tuned in to the concrete 3rd dimensional reality that surrounds you but also to the subtle information that may take the form of a gut feeling or a deep knowing.

Now read the definition of Mid-Consciousness below and notice how your understanding of it's meaning has deepened.

How is Mid-Consciousness Different?

During traditional meditation you have your eyes closed and as soon as you open them and begin interacting with your environment, the effect fades away. With mid consciousness you can not only function and interact with the world, but you can even use this interaction to deepen your desired state.

The Mid-Consciousness exercises do not require any techniques to be done before hand. There is no previous skill level or learning required. If you do the exercises in this book you can reduce your stress, think more clearly, eliminate stress related headaches and sleeping problems. You will be able to feel great even when bad things are going on in your life. Though not necessary, starting in a relaxed, centered and connected state has been shown to improve results. The exercises in the first two chapters guide you into such a state.

The Getting Present and Grounding techniques taught in this book originate from the teachings of Louis Bostwick founder of the Berkeley Psychic Institute (BPI). They were passed down to me by David Morelli who learned them from Rt. Rev. Mary Bell Nyman, Director of the Psychic Horizons Center in Boulder Colorado. As techniques are passed down each individual consciously or unconsciously adds their personal flavor to them. Despite not originating from Mid-Consciousness the first two exercises in this book are intentionally flavored with it.

If you are an experienced meditator you might be tempted to skip the exercises until chapter three. Instead, I invite and encourage you to do these exercises as they provide the fastest and best way I have experienced so far to get present and grounded.

Exercise One
Getting Present

Why Exercises?

The goal of this book is to teach you how to shift into Mid-Consciousness at will. Reading the material provides the mind with the facts and information it needs to buy in to the concepts. The exercises give you the experience and conditioning you need to be able to enter a Mid-Conscious state at will.

When a football player trains he spends many hours each day working on his body, strengthening his muscles, increasing his endurance, and doing drills over and over until he can execute the patterns without thinking about them. However, he also trains his mind, studying the playbook, techniques on how to block, catch or throw the ball, etc.

Just like the football player must be physically and mentally fit to excel at his sport, you must provide your mind with both the information and the training it needs in order to enjoy the benefits of Mid-Consciousness.

.

Have Trouble Reading and Doing Exercises?

In the past I (Hale) have often found myself frustrated trying to read and remember the steps to a meditation while attempting to meditate. I found that having a friend read the steps to me or recording myself reading them made things much easier. If you are like me then you will be excited to know that you can download audio versions of all the exercises in this book from the How To Feel Great Now website. Join our reader mailing list now to get free access to them and other content specifically designed for you. It's our gift to you for purchasing this book.

http://www.htfgn.com/readertools

The guided versions of the exercises available online are not identical to the ones in this book and may be updated from time to time so make sure you join our mailing list and don't miss out on these updates. The same results are achieved whether you read and walk yourself through the exercises or listen to the audio versions. We recommend trying both to see what works best for you. What is important is that you do the exercises. We have not heard of a single person who dramatically improved their life by simply reading this book (or any book for that matter). It takes action to translate knowledge into results.

We highly recommend using a notebook or journal to track your progress throughout this book. Some of the shifts you will experience will be subtle. Journaling as directed in the exercises will provide you with the validation your mind may need later and ensure you notice all the positive shifts. Remember to record the date and time of each journal entry, as it will be valuable information when you later review your entries.

We want you to be successful in reducing stress and feeling great all the time so we are making the PDF version of the "Feel Great Now Journal" available to you absolutely free. It has the questions from the each exercise with plenty of space to write your answers. You will receive it you when you join our mailing list at:

http://www.htfgn.com/readertools

So join us right now. Print the Journal, do the first exercise, and watch your stress levels drop.

Getting Present

1. **Record How You Feel** - Notice how you feel and write your answers to the following questions in your journal:

   a. What sensations or feelings are you experiencing?

   b. How do you feel about yourself?

   c. How do you feel about other people?

   d. How do you feel about the future?

2. **Prepare** - When you are done journaling turn the page in your journal and put your pen down so that you will be ready to record your results afterwards.

3. **Relax** - Take a deep breath. Hold it for a few seconds then let it out allowing your body to relax.

4. **Close Your Eyes**

5. **Gather Attention** - Imagine that you could gather up all your attention, right here, right now, in this moment as if you could just collect up the memories or attention that you have on this day, anything that has already happened, just imagine you could collect it up in this moment in the center of your head.

6. **Gather Scattered Attentions** - Imagine there is a magnet in the center of your head that would easily and effortlessly pull in any attentions that you have scattered around.

7. **Gather Past Attentions** - Now allow the magnet to draw to it any attentions from the past. Anywhere you have left your energy in the past, just imagine the magnet pulling it in, right here right now in the center of your head. Any attention that is stuck on childhood experiences, your teenage years etc. allow the magnet to bring them present right here right now in the center of your head.

8. **Gather Future Attentions** - Remember that the only time you can do anything is right now, and with that awareness in this moment, allow the magnet to draw in any place your attention is in the future on things that might happen, that you hope

will happen and on things you hope won't happen, just bring them all present right here, right now.

9. **Cleaning Attentions** - Now imagine that you have a scrub brush and you can brush away any of the clutter in the center of your head that is no longer serving you. Just allow those thoughts and emotions, anything at all that is not in your highest good to be brushed away.

10. **Notice How You Feel** - Do you feel cleaner, lighter or more present? What other sensations or feelings are you experiencing?

11. **Become Present** - Arrive fully right here, right now, in this moment, in your present location in space and time.

12. **Release Worries** - Take another deep breath hold it for a few seconds then let it out releasing all your cares and worries.

13. **Open Your Eyes.** - When you are ready open your eyes.

14. **Record How You Feel** - Notice how you feel and write your answers to the following questions in your journal:

    a. What sensations or feelings are you experiencing?

b. How do you feel about yourself?

c. How do you feel about other people?

d. How do you feel about the future?

e. What feels different than before?

I advise you not to go back and review what you wrote before the exercise at this time. Sometimes after clearing energies (thought patterns, emotions, stuck attention, crystallizations, etc.) focusing your attention on what was cleared can allow it back in. This is why I do not recommend reviewing how you were previously feeling especially right after you have cleared something. Often when something is freshly cleared you may have difficulty being neutral around it. Also, as time passes your body gets more used to not having whatever energies you cleared around and then the chance of you reattaching to that energy and popping back into old patterns is far less.

Chapter Two
The Realms of Consciousness

Before continuing there are a few more definitions that we want to share with you so that you can better understand the realms of consciousness:

Consciousness is the state of awareness of which you are in real-time. Your mind, body and spirit are all present working together to fulfill a desired task.

Thought Forms are patterns of thoughts in humans that are so ingrained that they are real no matter what truth is. They are as fictional and often as amusing as Dr. Seuss's critters. Often it is easier to recognize them in others. When we see an irrational or unusual behavior or reaction in someone a thought form is usually involved. It is either our thought form or theirs or both in action.

As humans we treasure our creations whether they are good or bad for they are familiar and we like the familiar.

The good news is we can consciously create thought forms that bias us to act or respond in a desired manner instead of falling prey to those we unconsciously created.

Attention is what one is focusing on. Focused thoughts use energy to produce emotion. When you have your attention on something and are judging it then your emotions are swayed one way or another. Literally "A Tension" is caused. If you are able to have your attention on something and not be judging it then you are in allowing.

Allowing is attention with no judgment and therefore no emotional attachment

Conscientiousness is an active state of mindfulness that focuses attention on a task using both the mind and the heart.

Knowing the above definitions you can now comprehend the realms of waking consciousness which include six distinct states: Unconsciousness, 1st Consciousness, 2nd Consciousness, 3rd Consciousness, 4th Consciousness and 5th Consciousness. These are states of awareness that we shift through during the day (except for unconsciousness), not components of the mind like conscious, subconscious, preconscious, or unconscious. Note also that these are waking states as opposed to sleeping states which are not covered in this book.

Realm of Unconsciousness

Unconsciousness is the state of being knocked out and non-responsive to environmental stimuli. This is not a sleeping or dreaming state but something deeper. It can be induced by a physical trauma like a blow to the head or oxygen deprivation. Fortunately, this is not a normal state for humans to be in. There is not much useful that one can consciously do from this state and it is covered here mainly for completeness. However, some people have out of body or near death experiences such as going to heaven or hell in the unconscious state so it can sometimes induce powerful shifts in certain individuals.

Realm of 1st Consciousness

This refers to primitive brain functions such as fight or flight. When you snap your hand back from touching a hot stove, when a tiger in the jungle or a thug on the street confronts you and you take immediate action to preserve your life, you are in 1st Consciousness. A gut reaction, where you have a physical sensation in response to a stimulus is another example.

Mothers who perform amazing feats like lifting a car to save their child were in 1st Consciousness. While 1st Consciousness is a powerful state to be in and was instrumental in our survival as hunters & gathers, it was intended to be experienced only occasionally and for short periods. Feeling stressed is an expression of this state as the fight & flight response is turned on due to imagined threats like deadlines or other events that might happen in the future.

Realm of 2nd Consciousness

You experience 2nd Consciousness when you are going through the motions or on autopilot. When in 2nd Consciousness you are not paying attention or present to what you are doing. Have you ever driven to work and had no recall of how you got from your home to your office. Maybe you were lost in thought, jamming out to some tunes, putting on your makeup, or eating a gluten free muffin and the driving somehow took care of itself. Once I (Hale) was driving down a windy road in a suburb of Atlanta Georgia and discovered that my radio had lost all its presets. I set all six presets and looked up to discover myself perfectly on course, stopped at a red light in the left turn lane with my turn signal on. I had no recollection of driving down the windy road, turning on my blinker or stopping at the light. This example also illustrates that we can be in more than one realm of consciousness at a time as the driving was in 2nd Consciousness and setting the presets on my radio was in 3rd Consciousness. In addition it is also possible to be doing multiple things in the same consciousness level at the same time. For example as I was driving and setting the radio presets, I was also breathing.

A habitual, preprogrammed, or reactive response is another form of 2nd Consciousness. Do you ever react to your children, your spouse, or a co-worker and then wonder why you behaved in that manner? It is because the same pattern is repeating itself due to synaptic programming. You are in 2nd Consciousness when something triggers you. When you have the thought "There he goes again." or "She always does that." you are in 2nd consciousness. You have identified the pattern in the other and are responding to it with your conditioned response. A lot of time I believe I'm acting out of free will (3rd consciousness) but later realized that I was actually reacting on autopilot instead of responding. Applying introspection by asking yourself questions like, "Why did I do that?" can help to analyze your behavior.

When used properly, 2nd Consciousness is extremely beneficial because it allows us to automate repetitive tasks. We can get things done without having to put our conscious attention on them. However, it also allows us to tune out and not be aware of our life. Looking back, days, weeks, months or even years may of passed by and we wonder where the time went. When was the last time you felt really alive? You were probably at least in 3rd consciousness then.

Realm of 3rd Consciousness

Being here and now, present in this moment, and in active thinking are ways in which we are in 3rd consciousness. We take in what is happening and rather than reacting we participate and create what comes next.

This state has an increased aliveness when compared to 2nd Consciousness. Instead of reacting to my son "doing it again", I can be with the behavior, allowing this unique moment to unfold as it does and to take appropriate action. There is a freedom here to act and flow in the moment which allows a more loving and compassionate response to emerge.

When you did the first exercise you shifted some of your attention into 3rd Consciousness. That was the intention behind the getting present exercise. Can you remember a moment when you were fully present? Have you ever had a close call or near miss? For example, you may have slammed on the breaks to avoid hitting the car in front of you or swerved to avoid an obstacle in the road. Do you remember how alive you felt afterward? Just being in 3rd Consciousness is amazing. Unfortunately, for most of us, it takes an unusual event just to get fully present. The good news is that the Mid-Consciousness techniques allow you to easily experience any desired state.

Realm of 5th Consciousness

Yes, I intentionally skipped 4th Consciousness. because it is easier to describe after explaining 5th Consciousness which is the realm of higher consciousness. People often experience it during meditation, sitting still with their eyes closed. However, during a moment of awe, when you feel deeply connected to nature or a loved one, you are also experiencing 5th Consciousness. Most people find it difficult to reach this state on demand. Even those who meditate regularly and can routinely get there typically cannot sustain this level of consciousness once they open their eyes and begin interacting with the world.

In the near miss example previously described in 3rd Consciousness, if you were left with a sense of awe, gratitude or everything being right in the world, that was an additional 5th Consciousness component.

Realm of 4th Consciousness

This is Mid-Consciousness or being in between 3rd and 5th Consciousness. More accurately, the boundary between 3rd and 5th Consciousness has dissolved and your entire mind is acting together in a synchronized and cooperative state. While in this state you are able to be fully present in the moment, but also connected to all that is in a heightened state of awareness. An athlete who is "in the zone" is in this state. When an artist paints, a musician plays, a writer writes, or an actor performs, and they feel totally immersed in what they are doing and totally alive doing it, they are in Mid-Consciousness. This state of consciousness is not only pleasurable to experience, but also useful in reprogramming the brain because in this state you have the ability to consciously access and alter the subconscious mind.

It is entirely possible to be in 3rd and 5th Consciousness but not in 4th. The near miss scenario is often an example of this. We feel alive and present (3rd Consciousness) and also have a euphoric sense of awe (5th Consciousness), but each feeling is distinct and separate. The wall between the conscious and subconscious is intact and we know this because there is no ability to consciously intensify the feeling of awe.

Shifting Between Realms

Now let's play with some realms. Take a deep breath and let it out. Notice that before you took that breath you were breathing but it was in 2nd Consciousness. Your 3rd Consciousness awareness was most likely focused on reading this book. As you took the breath awareness of breathing was brought into 3rd Consciousness, but by the time you read this sentence you are probably not aware of how many breaths transpired after the deep breath. That is how effortlessly and fluidly we shift between states and how unaware we usually are of the transition.

We are typically in multiple realms of consciousness at the same time and the percentage of our attention that is in each state typically swings wildly from moment to moment while we are active.

I (Hale) have even been in unconscious, 1^{st,} 2nd, and 3rd Consciousness all at the same time. Around 10 years ago, I had the flu and left work early. During the drive home, I noticed that my vision was dropping in and out, kind of like an online video skipping from one still image to another freeze frame every few seconds. This indicated that part of me was unconscious some of the time. I was also in fight or flight (1st Consciousness) as I had to get home before I passed out. I was driving on autopilot (2nd Consciousness) except for the moments just after a visual blackout where a course correction was required. I felt awful and some of my awareness was constantly on how bad I felt (3rd Consciousness). Fortunately I made it home safely and went straight to bed.

Assessing Your State

In the first exercise when you noticed how you felt and wrote down answers to questions in your journal, you were assessing your state. Knowing how you feel is the first step in the Mid-Consciousness technique.

State refers to the evaluation of your person at the body, emotional, and spiritual levels.

Mid-Consciousness allows you to be in control of your state. You can use the techniques to shift from one state to another. If you are feeling annoyed and angry and you desire to instead feel peaceful, you can make the shift. I invite you to notice how your state changes as you do the following grounding exercise.

Exercise Two
Grounding

If it has been more than an hour since you did the first exercise or you do not feel present, do step one below then do steps two through eleven of exercise one on page 25 Then continue with step five below. If you downloaded the guided exercises, there are separate audios for grounding alone, and for getting present and grounding combined (See Exercise one, on page 25 for directions on how to download the audio files.)

1. **Record How You Feel -** Start by assessing your state. Notice how you feel physically mentally and spiritually. Write your answers to the following questions in your journal:

   a. What sensations or feelings are you experiencing?

   b. How do you feel about yourself?

   c. How do you feel about other people?

   d. How do you feel about the future?

2. **Prepare -** When you are done journaling put your pen down and turn the page in your journal so that a blank

page is showing and you will be ready to record your results after you finish the exercise.

3. **Close Your Eyes**

4. **Relax** - Receive a deep breath, arriving right here right now and hold your breath for a few seconds then let it out.

5. **Deepen Into This Moment.** - Receive a few more breaths. Allow each breath to pull you into this moment, so you can be more present, more alert more alive and also more focused and more centered.

6. **Grounding Cord** - Imagine you have a grounding cord starting at the base of your hips and extending straight down all the way down to the center of the earth. It may look like a laundry chute, a large tube, or even a beam of light. Allow the cord to be as wide as or wider than your hips and be the same width all the way down. Imagine that this cord allows you to easily and effortlessly release anything that is no longer serving you.

7. **Add Gravity** - Enable gravity in your grounding cord so that anything you release will simply drop all the way down to the center of the earth to be recycled in its molten core.

8. **Add Suction** - In addition, allow your grounding cord to have a mild suction, like a vacuum cleaner hose, so that anything hanging around your grounding cord that is not in your highest and greatest good will be sucked out and returned to the center of the earth.

9. **Create an Energy Magnet.** - Now imagine that you have a powerful magnet in your right hand and that this magnet will easily and effortlessly pull out all energy that is no longer serving you.

10. **Collect Stuck Energy** - Wave the magnet all around your body allowing it to collect up any stuck energy that is hanging around. Anything that you are ready to let go of. Then drop the magnet down the grounding cord.

11. **Repeat 9 & 10** - Repeat the last two steps a few times. Try focusing on different areas of the body. People often have trapped energy in their head and gut so make sure to go over those areas thoroughly.

12. **Connect to This Moment** - Also allow the grounding cord to solidly anchor you in the present moment in time and allow it to help you to feel more physically connected to the space you are in.

13. **Persist the Grounding Cord** - Set the intention that the grounding cord will remain intact and operational for the remainder of the day.

14. **Become Present** - Arrive fully present, right here, right now, in this moment, alert, awake and feeling fantastic.

15. **Open Your Eyes** - When you are ready open your eyes.

16. **Record How You Feel** - Finish by assessing your state. Notice how you feel physically, mentally, emotionally and spiritually. Write your answers to these questions in your journal.

   a. What sensations or feelings are you experiencing?

   b. How do you feel about yourself?

   c. How do you feel about other people?

   d. How do you feel about the future?

Now that you have the grounding cord in place you can easily release anything that comes up.

Chapter Three
Patterns & Programming

- Where are you right now?

- Not your physical body, but where is your mind?

You are probably in a static state. Most of the time, most people are in the 2nd Realm of Consciousness doing things automatically. They are in their trenches – going about their day - no new thoughts or ideas. Are you stuck repeating your old patterns? Since you are reading this book you either have relatively few deep trenches in your mind or a strong desire to change one of more of them. Either way you are in the right place. We now invite you to jump out of the trenches in your mind. Lets explore how your trenches were built, their purpose and how to consciously build new trenches that guide your mind in the direction you desire.

How New Neural Pathways Are Created

I (Janá) am from the woods of East Texas. This is the story of how your mind learns new ideas. When you encounter a new concept such as Mid-Consciousness, your mind is very resistant. The idea bounces around your mind for there is no trail to go on.

It is the same in the deep undergrowth of East Texas. To form a path the smallest animals of the woods push though the bramble. Your first new thought is like a rabbit pushing its way through this undergrowth. It is hard and briars are tearing at you but you are resilient and continue on blazing a path through this underbrush. It was a new thought and it was hard but now that a new thought pattern has been built. You look back and notice the rabbit path you created and now you can run like a rabbit on the path. It is only a small path but it is much better and easier than blazing a new trail.

As armadillo and possums use the path it is broadened. These bigger thoughts and ideas use the existing path because they are similar in nature, build upon or are in resonance with the first new thought. It is easier to use an existing pathway than to build an entirely new one.

Soon deer will pass making it deeper and clearer. People now can walk on this path and soon find it easier to pave the way for a road and eventually it becomes a highway. This is how we train our brain, how we create new ways of thinking. It illustrates how every human makes new thoughts and adopts new ways of thinking.

- Do you see how difficult it is to make a new

path for a new thought?

As the road continues to be used, it starts to become a trench. Deeper and deeper it becomes as more repetitive thoughts flow through it. Eventually it is the Grand Canyon and it takes a lot of effort to climb out of it. This is neither god or bad, it simply is the way it works. William Shakespeare said it a little more eloquently "There is nothing good or bad, but thinking makes it so." If these thought patterns are serving you in creating the life you desire then you may think of them as good or positive, if they hinder you, you may think of them as bad or negative.

This process illustrates how people become set in their ideas and concepts. Their thought patterns crystallize and their thinking becomes rigid and unable to move in new directions.

The Power of Symbols

There are connectors in the brain that connect things. Like old crayons in a box can make you think of your school. The image or maybe the smell is the link that activates the pathway in your brain bringing back a flood of memories. In the example above, the old crayons were the symbol that brought back a previous state. This is the power of symbols: They can be used to connect you with a state.

You are already familiar with a lot of symbols for example the flag of your country, the swastika, the cross, the Star of David, the pentagram, etc. Be aware that the same symbol can be interpreted differently by different people. Notice how you felt as you thought about each of the symbols mentioned. I deliberately included symbols that would bring about a variety of feelings in you. Note also that you may be neutral and entirely uninfluenced by some of the symbols and have strong feelings toward others.

In addition, a symbol does not have to be visual, the sound of your national anthem, rain on a tin roof, or your favorite song are all audible symbols. The smell of your mothers cooking, the taste of your favorite desert, or the sensation of stroking a velvet cloth can all be powerful symbols. Anything that allows you to tune back into a moment in time where you experienced a particular state is also makes a powerful symbol. For example thinking of my first car (an ugly old olive green 66 Buick Special) brings me (Hale) back to the terrible loneliness and sense not belonging that I experienced in high school. The symbol that works best to connect you with a specific state is the one that most easily brings you the feeling of that state. Pick something that is meaningful to you.

Trenches in the Mind

Some people continue going deeper and deeper into their patterns creating trenches in their minds, and rarely have any new thoughts. They become stuck in their Grand Canyons either enjoying rafting down the Colorado River or dreading each bump and turn. The good news is that even a thought pattern as mighty as the Grand Canyon can be easily and quickly changed. It took over 4 million years for the Grand Canyon to form, but today with our modern machinery we can divert the river by building a dam in a few years. Mid-Consciousness is the modern machinery of thought that allows you to create new pathways in your brain.

Mid-Consciousness can be thought of as a little adventure for the brain on a new path in a new direction. Mid-Consciousness pairs the difficulty of forging a new path with the ease of driving down the road, thereby allowing progress to be made as quickly as possible.

We want to connect you now with a whole new way of thinking. To think of teaching your mind to build a path that allows you to live in Higher Consciousness on a daily basis is hard. So don't worry about that. Instead take a rabbit hop: simply turn the page and do the exercise.

Enjoy your new state.

Repeat, InJoy   (The spelling of enjoy is intentional.)

Repeat...

Exercise Three
Explore Your State

In Mid-Consciousness you will learn to change your state at will. This exercise demonstrates one way to change your state and is useful when you want to increase or decrease the intensity of an aspect of your state.

1. **Record How You Feel** - Start by assessing your state. Notice how you feel physically mentally and spiritually. Write your answers to these questions in your journal.

   a. What sensations or feelings are you experiencing?

   b. Are you happy, sad, angry, bored, lonely, peaceful or something else?

2. **Prepare** - When you are done journaling turn the page and put your pen down so that you will be ready to record your results afterwards.

3. **Multiple States** - Notice that you can be in more than one state at a time.

4. **Choose Your Symbol** - Now pick a symbol for your current state. If you are in multiple states pick one of

them. Draw, doodle or write your symbol in your journal.

5. **Overlay Your Symbol** - Overlay your symbol on your state. Imagine you could rubber stamp your state with your symbol so that they are linked.

6. **Allowing** - Allow yourself to be in the state, simply accepting it.

7. **Dimmer Switch** - Now imagine you have a dimmer switch, which controls the intensity of your state instead of the brightness of a light bulb. Imagine that the range on your dimmer switch goes from zero percent (or off) to 100% (or full expression).

8. **Dimmer Switch Setting** Notice the level your dimmer switch is currently set at and record this in your journal.

9. **Establish Control** - Know that you can decide to feel more or less of your state. That it is totally under your control.

10. **Turn It Up.** - Using your dimmer switch, turn up the intensity of your state. Notice if it gets harder to turn up or gets stuck at a certain setting.

11. **Assess Your State** - Notice how you feel as you turn up the intensity of your state.

12. **Eliminate the Effort** - If it is taking a lot of effort to change your state, simply switch off the effort. Simply allow it to be effortless as manipulating energy is actually effortless.

13. **Turn It Down** - Now try turning down your state. Is there a level at which it becomes uncomfortably low?

14. **Final Setting** - Now set your dimmer switch to the level that will best support you in going through the next few hours.

15. **Become Present** - Arrive fully present, right here, right now, in this moment, alert, awake and feeling fantastic.

16. **Open Your Eyes** - When you are ready allow your state to remain at the level you set it as you open your eyes.

17. **Record How You Feel** - Journal about what you learned and how you felt as you changed your state.

Double Check - Now check the level on your dimmer switch. Did it change as you wrote in your journal? If it did you can set it back to the previous level or the level that feels best at this moment.

Bonus exercise: Exploring "Negative" Emotions

We all like to experience more joy, fulfillment, happiness, bliss etc. However, sometimes exploring states that we may judge as negative such as anger, sadness or jealousy create amazing shifts by providing a safe outlet for these states to express themselves. I invite you to find a safe place where you can hit your pillow, cry or yell without worrying about what others may think and repeat the explore your state exercise with one of your "negative" emotions.

As you turn up the intensity on negative emotions allow them to express and allow yourself to feel them fully. You may find it becoming harder and harder to find the negative emotion. I invite you treat yourself gently and lovingly while allowing the negative patterns to express themselves. When you have turned up the intensity to 100% and you can find no trace of the negative emotion, you have fully processed it. The energy associated with the negative emotion has been fully expressed and is no longer stuck in your body. If instead you turn down the volume on unpleasant emotions, it is like pushing a beach ball under water. You may feel good right now sitting on the submerged beach ball, but at an inopportune moment it is sure to upset your balance by popping to the surface.

Chapter Four
Give Yourself Permission

We know that you genuinely want to change. If not you would have stopped reading this book long before you reached this page. You may perceive change as scary, think real change is not possible or even be excited about change. Regardless of how you feel about change, granting yourself permission to change will improve the process. Now let's explore how you can create the changes you desire in your life by exploring the answer to the following question:

What is the main thing that holds you back from achieving your dreams?

Write your answer in your journal then turn the page.

57

- Did you answer "**belief**"?

You may believe that it is too hard, it will take too much time, it won't work, it won't be worth it, etc. Henry Ford said "If you think you can, or if you think you can't, either way, you're right" What Mr. Ford did not address, though he surely knew it, is that your thinking is based on both your conscious and subconscious beliefs.

We will tell you now that it is our internal beliefs that limit us, not our external circumstances. You may say "This is not true, it was not my fault that…" We do not ask that you to blindly believe what we tell you. In fact as a Scientist I (Hale) recommend you test and experiment with everything that you encounter and see if it holds true for you. We now invite you to consider two philosophies:

1. My thoughts, beliefs and actions are totally responsible for my current situation.

2. Someone else or something else is to blame for my current situation.

   - Which feels right to you?

If your thoughts, beliefs and actions are responsible for your current situation, then they can be changed and you are empowered to create positive changes in your life. However, if someone else or something else is to blame, you have limited or no control of changing their behavior or the situation.

In the past, I (Hale) often played the victim. Woe is me, look at all my problems! Can't you see I have all of this to deal with? Don't you feel sorry for me? I hid in my turtle shell, depressed, waited for the storm to blow over. However, instead of things getting better they got worse.

Now, I choose to believe that I control my destiny. Yes, my life is still far from perfect, but it is getting better. I feel that changing my beliefs about myself, from a victim of my circumstances to an empowered creator was the starting point for the shift in my external circumstances. Changing my beliefs led to taking positive actions in my life that created positive results.

So: How do you change your belief?

Pause here and write down your answer in your journal.

When I (Hale) asked this question at one of my live events I got the following answers:

- Reprogram the belief

- Cleanse – Get rid of the old stuff

- Have small successes and build on them to create bigger successes

- Change your consciousness

- Through being thankful and grateful

All of the answers above are good answers which speak toward methodology, action or the "how" of changing belief.

- But what exactly causes your belief to change?

There are two ways in which humans change their beliefs. They can either accumulate enough evidence or have an experience.

1. Accumulate enough evidence

Imagine that you live near a pond. Each day you watch the ducks swim and waddle around on the ground. Some even flap their wings, but you have never seen one fly. In fact, nobody in your town had ever seen a duck fly and you and everyone you know believes that ducks do not fly. Since you knew that most birds can fly and ducks are birds, you started doing research, reading books, encyclopedia articles, etc. At some point the evidence becomes overwhelming and you believe that ducks can fly. Depending on how deeply you hold the belief it may take a lot of time and research to change it or there may simply not be enough evidence available to sway you.

Ultimately, a thorough understanding of the inner workings may even lead the mind to an incorrect conclusion. For example, if you were to take two highly combustible elements and mix them together you would expect to get something explosive. However water is made of Hydrogen and Oxygen (both flammable gasses) and it not only does not ignite, but can be used to extinguish fire. So be careful of the "obvious" conclusions in your exploration of consciousness as the logical mind can often lead you down a false path.

2. Have an experience

Now imagine that you, a firm non-believer in ducks flying, are sitting by the same pond. You watch as a duck begins flapping its wings, takes off and flies away over the trees. In that moment your belief can change dramatically. It took less than a minute to experience a duck flying but now your belief has shifted so strongly that no amount of harassment by the townsfolk could ever shift your belief back. Or maybe after the duck flew away you thought, "I must have been seeing things" and sank back into the accepted reality where ducks don't fly.

This book uses both mechanisms to allow you to shift your beliefs: It provides both concepts and ideas for the mind that build evidence, and exercises which allow you to have an experience. Your experience will be uniquely yours and may or may not resemble others experiences. However, we find that there are common elements that many people experience. Therefore we will describe some of these experiences in this book.

Effortless Movement

While I (Hale) was living in Hilo, Hawaii, I practiced a Japanese martial art called Aikido. Once, in a one hour class, the instructor decided that we were going to do 1000 sword strikes. Each of the five participants would count in turn from one to ten in Japanese providing the cadence to which we all swung our swords. I was fourth and by the time it was my turn to count I remember being exhausted. I thought "Only 30 strikes and we were going to do 1000! How could this be possible?"

Then something happened but I did not notice it at the time. What I was keenly aware of on my next turn to count was that I could not remember what came after three. Yes it was in Japanese, but I could not remember "four" in

English either. I loudly but indistinctly mumbled something that probably did not resemble the next six numbers. During this counting attempt my next awareness happened. All of a sudden my sword was heavy and I was exhausted again. After counting, I began to relax back into the rhythm of striking to the count and in that moment I noticed the shift.

All of a sudden it was effortless. As if the sword and my body were weightless. Then as it grew close to time for me to count again, I began searching for the numbers. As my attention focused there, my sword became heavy and my arms became tired. I was able to count better but still had some difficulty. Throughout the rest of the class, over 600 strikes, I navigated between the peaceful and wonderful state of effortless movement and effortful and weary state of being able to count, think logically, and analyze what was going on with me. Sometimes I would go too far and count perfectly but become tremendously tired, almost unable to lift my sword. Other times I would stay too relaxed with almost effortless movement and would mumble through some numbers.

At the time, my mind could not understand what happened. Now I believe that this was one of my first Mid-Consciousness experiences, where my conscious and subconscious mind were synchronized. In addition, universal energy was flowing in and powering my movements. I felt really wonderful for many hours after the class was over.

Can You Commit?

- So now the question becomes are you willing to move, to change your beliefs?

- Are you willing not just to have an experience but to be open to the full gamut of what the experience provides?

In Chapter Three we explained why resistance to new patterns is typical. This is why so many self-help books sit unread in dusty bookcases. You say that you can move but we find so many that do not. They are pinned in a work cycle that controls their every move from the time they wake until the time they fall exhausted in bed. They look for pleasure or time for themselves and they find none.

- Are you one of them?

- Did you really sign up for this or is it just a bad dream?

- How can you tell?

- What can you do about it?

Your boss, partner, and children have needs too. You

cannot change them. You can only change you.

- Decide that you are worth the change.
- Decide to give yourself permission to change.

Now do the exercise on the following page to anchor this decision into your mind.

Exercise Four
Through The Gate

If you have not done the first three exercises, go back and do them first. This exercise builds upon the foundation of getting present and grounding introduced in the first two exercises.

See Exercise One on page 25 for directions on how to download the mp3 audio file for this meditation.

In step eight of this exercise I mention "the white light of the Holy Spirit". I use this exact language because it is the highest vibrational choice that resonates with me that I am currently aware of. You can substitute "Source" or whatever concept of divinity you hold for "Holy Spirit" as these terms may resonate more with you and therefore produce a higher vibration for you. If you do not believe in a higher power try substituting "Love" or "the Universe". In step nine you can substitute "Higher Self" for "Divine Energy". Do whatever works for you instead of getting caught up in the wording. You have permission to change the exercises in any way that works for you in your personal practice of these exercises.

1. **Assess Your State** - Notice how you feel physically, mentally, emotionally and spiritually. Write down how you feel in your journal.

Prepare - When you are done journaling turn the page in your journal and put your pen down so that you will be ready to record your results afterwards.

Close Your Eyes

Tune In - Receive a deep breath, arriving right here right now, hold it for a few seconds then let it out.

Deepen Into This Moment - Receive a few more breaths. Allow each breath to pull you into this moment, so you can be more present, more alert, more alive while also being more focused and more centered.

Center Yourself - Gather your attention in the center of your head (See Exercise 1, p. 25)

Ground - Connect your grounding cord (See Exercise 2, p. 43)

Fill in With light - Allow the white light of the Holy Spirit to surround, fill, and protect you in this moment and to remain throughout this exercise and even through the rest of your day.

Flow the Light - Allow this white light to flow in from above and flow through your body and down the grounding cord. Like a river of white light this Divine energy picks up any energies that are not serving you and carries them down the grounding cord to the center of the earth.

Wash With Light Now bring your attention to your head. Allow this light to wash away any thoughts, concepts, ideas, and or beliefs that are swimming around in your head which are not serving you in becoming the truest, greatest and most amazing version of you possible.

New Path Permission - You have permission now to create a new path in your mind. Repeat after me out loud: "I give myself permission to create a new path in my mind."

Gate Permission - You have permission to create a gate in your life that will create ease. Repeat after me out loud "I have permission to create a gate in my life that creates ease."

Permission to Pass Through - You have permission to go through the gate at will. Repeat out loud "I give myself permission to go through the gate at will."

Create Your Gate - Now visualize your gate ahead of you. Notice how your gate looks. It may look any way you want from an old rusty gate on a farm, to a fancy door, to a star gate. Allow it to have a magical property that creates ease for anyone passing through it.

Create the Path - See a path leading up to and extending through and beyond your gate.

Walk Toward Your Gate - Visualize yourself standing on this path and begin walking toward your gate.

Walk up to Your Gate – Visualize yourself arriving at the gate. If you need to open the gate do that now and leave it open.

Through the Gate - When you are ready, step through your gate allowing it to create ease as you pass through it.

Assess Your State - Notice how you are feeling. Do things seem easier?

Loop the Path - Now curve the path beyond the gate back on itself so that it connects to the start of the path and forms a circle.

"Ease" Intention - Allow your gate to create ease each time you go through it.

Through the Gate Again - Now continue walking on the path until you come to the gate and pass through it again creating more ease.

Notice Increasing Easiness - Notice that it took a little time to set up this gate the first time, and it was even easier to go through it a second time.

Through the Gate Again and Again - Pass through the gate at least five more times noticing that things become easier each time. You may want to shrink the size of your path or allow yourself to fly above it at the speed of light. All this creates more ease by improving the visualization.

Save Button - When you feel complete, imagine that there is a save button floating above and to the left of your gate.

Save the Gate - Click the save button and allow it to commit the gate to memory, to a permanent space in your mind. You can easily pull your gate back up anytime you would like things to be easier. All you have to do is think of your gate and it will appear.

Become Present - Arrive fully present, right here, right now, in this moment, alert, awake and feeling fantastic.

Open Your Eyes - When you are ready allow your state to remain at the level you set it as you open your eyes.

Record How You Feel - Journal about what you learned and how you felt as you created ease.

Chapter Five
Can You Move?

Physical movement in humans is important. Many have become still because of their jobs or health reasons. Now move with me. What movements feel good to you? Twirling, stretching, bending, laying down, standing, swinging, leaning, scratching, rubbing, singing, jumping, skipping, etc. I invite you to do it now. Make some movements and explore the sensations brought on through movement. We will do more physical movements in the exercise following this chapter.

Small children move a lot, and they learn a lot through movement. Movement is our natural learning style. It is hard for children when they go to school to sit and not move because there learning style has been movement. The sensation of movement is one of the keys to unlocking higher consciousness. This should not be surprising as when you look at how the universe operates it is full of motion. From the tiny electron whirling around the nucleus of an atom, to our earth revolving around the sun, to our sun revolving around the center of the Milky Way galaxy, physical motion is present everywhere.

When water flows it is a vital part of an ecosystem, but

when it sits, water becomes stagnant. We are mostly water, yet in modern society most of us spend the majority of our day at a desk and do not move our bodies much. We circle around the mall looking for a close parking spot to minimize the walk. Then we get home and sit in front of the TV. It is no wonder life seems dull: The excitement and joy we experienced as a child has faded. We often feel bored, trapped or stuck: This is what stagnation feels like.

One sunny Colorado morning I was driving down a small dirt road in Palmer Park. Suddenly upon rounding a curve a big red truck appeared out of nowhere and came barreling speedily toward me. I quickly swerved as far right as I could. He zoomed by somehow missing me on a road that was barely wide enough for two cars to pass. As soon as the truck had passed by I was filled with gratitude. Thank goodness he missed me. I was excited just to be alive (or at least to be uninjured). A few minutes later I reached my destination, parked, got out of the car and walked a few steps to behold the view of Colorado Springs below me, the Garden of the Gods Park ahead of me and a snow capped Pikes Peak Mountain towering above me. I had seen the view many times before, but this morning it was more alive, more vibrant, more 3D, than I had ever experienced it before.

After a few minutes of enjoying the view, my mind

began to ponder the reason why my experience was so different. There was nothing unusually great about the view that day. In fact a few weeks earlier I had experienced a beautiful sunset from this very spot that was far more spectacular. Obviously what was different was me. "But what about me?", I pondered. I concluded that it was a combination of the following two things:

- My mind was clear of all the usual clutter so I was present and in the moment

- I was full of gratitude

I did not realize it at the time but physical motion can be used to clear the mind just like the red truck did for me that morning. In addition, using the Mid-Consciousness visualizing techniques taught in this book, you can create and experience any feeling you desire such as feeling full of gratitude. This combination allows me to virtually recreate the state of consciousness I experienced that morning at will.

Have you ever had an amazing experience of being present, feeling alive or being in awe?

Would you like an easy way to create a similar experience whenever you desired?

If so you are reading the right book. Don't worry, there is no special ability required. Anybody that can read this book can learn to do it. All you need is the desire, the techniques in this book and a little practice.

There are many things that adults don't do any more that are so much fun. In fact, adults limit themselves so much and have so few things left and hardly any of them involve movement. I invite you to use movement as a way to break free.

You cannot be in a higher consciousness without the connections. Each exercise in this book that you do helps to establish a connection. When you get present you make a connection to the current moment. When you ground you make a connection to the earth which helps you to stabilize and to anchor you into your physical spot in the universe. When you explore your state you are connecting to your experience. In the next exercise you will use physical movement to make the connection to your body while it is moving in the 3rd Dimension.

Each connection is unique and important. They are taught sequentially in this book so that you can use each experience to build on the next. The order is not as important as learning addition before multiplication, but it is important to make each connection as they all work together to shape your experience.

Yes, some people spend many hours in meditation to get into higher consciousness and feel better. However, meditating for four hours to feel good for fifteen minutes is not productive. We doubt that you have many four-hour blocks of time each week and even if you did we do not think you would regularly use them for meditation. Instead, we wish you to move and feel better instantly. Once you feel the benefits of making intentional movements, it will be easy to add many brief movements into your day. You can intentionally walk, run, skip or even stand at the water cooler. In the bathroom you could turn around three times before flushing. This may sound silly but adding movement can greatly improve how you feel, especially when paired with an intention, as we will explain in Chapter Eight Pairing.

Your body wants to move, your mind wants to move, your spirit wants to move. Now move with us throughout your day. If you wake up to an alarm clock set it three minutes early. You probably won't even notice losing the three minutes of sleep. However, when you wake up, you now have three minutes of extra time that morning. Use them to lay in bed, stretching all your muscles, roll back and forth, wiggle your shoulders and toes, enjoying all the sensations.

As you get ready for work, notice each movement, from brushing your teeth to taking a shower. Can you add movements to some of your daily activities, such as dancing as you rinse the soap off your skin in the shower? Are there tasks that you do each day at work that you could add a little movement to?

Now challenge yourself to add one new activity daily, weekly or monthly. As you do this you will drop previous standing commitments that no longer serve you. We invite you to try it out and be creative.

Exercise Five
Move With Me

Can movement improve your mood? Try out the following exercise and test it out.

> *Make sure to do the exercises in a safe space. The spinning exercise can make you dizzy and you might bump into something or stumble and fall. Know your limitations and don't harm yourself.*

If you have any physical limitations that prevent you from doing any of the exercises below, feel free to substitute other exercises. Try a combination of gross motor exercises such as walking, skipping, or jumping and fine motor exercises such as wiggling toes, opening and closing your hand or taking deep breaths. Even if you are paralyzed from the neck down you can probably blink your eyes and move your lips. If you are not able to do the exercises below, you can receive similar benefits by simply visualizing yourself doing the exercises because the mind does not know the difference between imagined and real events.

1. **Assess Your State** – In Exercise Three, p. 53, you learned to assess your state. That is all that is required for this step. Simply connect with how you are feeling in the moment. This is referred to as your initial state. Notice how you feel physically, mentally, emotionally, and spiritually. Write down how you feel in your journal.

2. **Sweeping Motion**

    - Standing with your feet shoulder width apart and hands reaching high above your head, sweep your hands down to your toes allowing your head and upper body to follow

    - Pause for a second or two and extend the stretch try to touch your shoes

    - Then sweep your hands up to the sky allowing your head and upper body to follow

    - Pause there reaching high as if you could reach the sky or even bend back slightly getting a good stretch

    - Repeat the process three times

3. **Assess Your State** - Notice how you feel after doing sweeping motions and remember how you felt during it. Journal about your experience.

4. **Tapping**

- Start by taking your three middle fingers on your right hand and tap the inside of your left wrist.

- Try different tapping speeds. I (Hale) tap at about two taps per second. What speed feels best for you?

- You can play with the intensity of the tap. Too hard may feel jarring and too soft may feel itchy or tingly.

- When it feels natural, or after about 30–45 seconds switch hands so that you are tapping with the three middle fingers of your left hand on the inside of your right wrist.

- When it feels natural, or after about 30–45 seconds, try tapping different points on your body. Some places I like to tap are the center of the head between the eyebrows, under the arm on the bone just below the armpit, knees, ankles, bottom of the feet, palms, and the center of the chest.

- For the next two - three minutes tap on different parts of your body. Feel free to alternate hands.

5. **Assess Your State** - Notice how you feel after tapping and remember how you felt during it. Did tapping with your right hand seem different than with your left hand? Journal about your experience.

6. **Spinning in Place** – This can be done standing up or in a chair that swivels. In both cases look around and make sure there are no sharp objects to bump into, nothing to knock over and no hard or dangerous surfaces to fall down on.

   - Spin around in a circle until you start to get dizzy

   - Stop and stand or sit still

7. **Observe Your Surroundings** - Notice how the room looks right after you stop spinning. Is it still spinning? Does it seem to rock back & forth? Did you spin clockwise or counterclockwise? Journal about your experience.

8. **Assess Your State** - Notice how you feel physically, mentally, emotionally, and spiritually. How do you feel different than before? Write about your experience in your journal.

Chapter Six
The Mid-Consciousness Experience

Mid-Consciousness is not to intended be used in any activity in which hesitation, slow response time, and or not paying attention could result in bodily harm or property damage such as but not limited to driving a car or operating heavy machinery.

The technique taught in the next exercise is the core of Mid-Consciousness. It allows you to experience any state you desire. You can use it to experience any feeling you have had in the past. You can even use it to experience a feeling that you have never experienced before. While, we had an idea of what Divine Bliss might feel like, as you probably do, we certainly had not experienced it before using Mid-Consciousness to create it.

One beautiful, crisp and clear Saturday morning I (Hale) loaded up my car with my speakers, projector, screen, computer and everything else needed to put on my first Mid-Consciousness Live Event. While driving from Colorado Springs to the Marriott Courtyard in Denver, I had a powerful experience of Divine Bliss. It lasted for almost 30 minutes! Tears were streaming out of my eyes and I had to wipe them frequently. I flipped my tie over my shoulder to avoid getting it wet. There were periods where I was silent, other times it sounded like I was crying or wailing, and other times I was laughing. At one point I remember the sound I was making transitioning fluidly from crying to laughing. The feeling was amazing throughout the experience and at the end I was left with a deep sense of peace. About 15 minutes later upon arriving at the Marriott, the parking lot was about ½ full, but the closest spot to the front door was waiting for me. This made unloading all my equipment really easy.

Have you ever flashed back to a traumatic experience from the past? Did you feel like you were reliving it even though you were in a completely different situation? Maybe there was one similarity that triggered the flashback or maybe the trigger was unconscious.

The story described above was my (Hale's) first Mid-Consciousness flashback. I had been practicing the techniques for a few months and had experienced Divine Bliss only about four times. That morning I was in a good mood, grateful for the beautiful day and excited about sharing Mid-Consciousness with the first group of people. On the drive I played an inspiring song and the music was the trigger that brought forth my experience of Divine Bliss. Right now as I write this, I am experiencing moments of Divine Bliss. Simply tuning back into that moment to write the story evoked the feeling within me.

Why does it seem easier to relive negative experiences than positive ones? It could be that they stand out more to you due to their intensity or that you have a filter running that makes them easier to see. If you reflect on your life, you can probably remember moments when you should have been sad, but were happy instead. In reality it is just as easy to relive a positive experience. If you have daydreamed, you were probably doing just that.

In Chapter Six we talked about making connections. Mid-Consciousness uses the following five connections to navigate you from what you are experiencing to what you desire to experience:

1. **The First Connection is Knowing Your State.** You have done the exercise of tuning in to how you are feeling. It is important to make the mind connections to where you are before you can go any place. Be in the now. When planning a trip you need to know the starting location before you can plan your route to your destination. Knowing and accepting your state: How you are feeling in the moment is the first step to changing it. You may not want to admit you are in

Kansas City and would prefer to depart from Florida for your Cruise to the Bahamas, but your detailed directions will be useless if you are not in the correct starting place.

2. **The Second Connection is to Your Destination.** Intending your state is like looking on a map and deciding where you want to go. You are the captain of your ship and can pick any destination. However, without a destination, you will drift where the tides of life take you.

3. **The Third Connection is to Allowing.** By allowing your emotions to take care of themselves, you are using the automation pathways in your brain. This is connecting with ease. Letting go of control and allowing the change to happen. This is like hiring a competent babysitter. You don't have to worry about your children while you are out on the town, because you know they are safe and being cared for. This frees you up to have a great time.

4. **The Fourth Connection is With Spiritual Transport Energy.** It allows you to energetically move from one state of being to another. To invoke this energy, the easiest and simplest way we use a symbol. In Exercise Three you used symbols to connect to your Existing State. In this exercise you

will use a symbol for your Desired State. Allowing the symbol to shift your state is like allowing a cruise ship to take you to your destination. You don't have to worry about how to get there, just board the ship or use the symbol in this case. You can also use symbols to move around from one place to another in space or time, or to join with source as will be discussed in future books.

5. **The Fifth Connection is With Your Intended State.** Feel the feelings, see, feel, hear, taste, smell and know your destination. Intend to be there or arrive. Solidify the experience. However, this is not about doing anything except starting the process. You do not visualize the process of changing, you start the process and it changes as if you were on the cruise ship and all you needed to do was tell the captain to depart and you immediately arrive at the destination.

Now that you understand the connections used to change how you are feeling you may be wondering "But how do I do that?" It's a simple five step process, which is explained in Exercise Six, page 89. It may seem like a long exercise the first time, as there is a lot of explanation on how to do each step, however, after you have done it a few times it will take you less than a minute.

Describing what you are going to do is a little like

explaining how to ride a bicycle. You won't fully understand the experience until you take your first ride. We invite you to do the next exercise and have your first experience.

Exercise Six
Experiencing Divine Bliss

First decide that you are deserving of a pleasurable experience. Now plan to be in Divine Bliss.

Each step is explained in detail first, as this helps alleviate any mental concerns that may arise during the exercise and might minimize your results. So first read and understand each step. You will be walked through the exercise after all steps are explained.

1. **Assess Your State** – In Exercise Three, p. 55, you learned to assess your state. That is all that is required for step one. Simply connect with how you are feeling in the moment. This is referred to as your initial state.

2. **Intend Your State** – Hold your Desired State in your mind. What do you want to experience, or how do you want to feel? For this exercise I invite you to choose Divine Bliss as your Intended State.

3. **Automate Your Initial State** – In Chapter Three, p. 47, we talked about automation. How people are often in the 2nd realm of consciousness doing things automatically. In this exercise we will use the human capacity for automation to create ease and to amplify

89

the desired results. In step three you simply let go of how you are feeling and allow it to take care of itself.

4. **Overlay Your Symbol** – Chose a symbol for your intended state and overlay it. In Chapter Three, p. 49, we talked about the power of symbols and how to choose good ones. If you are having trouble coming up with a symbol for Divine Bliss, just pick a symbol that connects you to it. Visualizing your symbol on top of your body and feeling it soaking into you, generally works well. However, there is not one right way to do this step, so feel free to experiment with what works best for you as you overlay your symbol.

Tip: Don't spend much time on step four. Many people try to use effort and force the symbol to change their state. Instead simply proceed to step five and allow automation to take care of the rest.

5. **Push Start** - Begin your transformation. In the fifth and final step you take the middle three fingers of your right hand and bring them together, then tap once on your forehead with the intention to start the process. This allows the transformation to automate. After the tap you simply relax and observe what happens. There is no need to guide it or force it. Allow it to occur effortlessly.

Tip: When you click play on your remote control, you expect your DVD player to play the movie. When you push the start, have the expectation that your state will shift. Instead of trying to force your state to shift, relax into it. Simply sit back and enjoy the experience like you are on a cruise and your every need is taken care of.

Mid-Consciousness Basic Exercise

You are now ready to do the exercise. Prepare to do this without interruptions. The Grounding and Getting Present exercises are not necessary, but doing them beforehand will usually enhance your experience. As you do step one below, recording your state in your journal will help you track the changes that occur. Remember to assign a level, either one to ten or a percentage for each component of your state. When you are done turn the page in your journal so that you will have a fresh page to write on and won't see your old state when you complete the exercise. It is best, at least initially, to keep your eyes closed from steps two through five, so do not interrupt the process to write anything down until after step five.

1. **Assess Your State** – Notice how you are feeling.

2. **Intend Your State** – Set the intention to be in Divine Bliss or whatever other state you desire

3. **Automate Your Initial State** – Let go of how you are feeling and allow it to take care of itself

4. **Overlay the Symbol for Your Intended State** – Relax and let the symbol do the work for you.

5. **Push Start** – Tap your forehead and allow yourself to transform into your intended state.

Watch or feel your state change. After a few seconds or sometimes as long as a few minutes you will feel like your state has stabilized and is no longer changing. At this point set the intention to retain your state as you open your eyes and then allow your eyes to gently open, while keeping your focus internal.

Record your state in your journal. Don't compare your current state to your previous state right now. Instead, turn the page in your journal once more and repeat the exercise. Do this at least two more times. You will often find that each time you do the exercise you connect or open into your desired state in a deeper way.

As you did the Mid-Consciousness basic exercise, did it seem like day dreaming? Yes, but instead of trying to work out problems you are raising your energy level. We invite you to be in this divine space by making it your special space. Feel the comfort and keep it sacred by not allowing any other things to be a part of your time here.

Chapter Seven
Movement and Meditation

In traditional meditation, your eyes are closed, your legs are crossed and you try to empty your mind of thoughts. This is time consuming, uncomfortable and quite difficult to do. In the high tech field, there is always something better and newer evolving. The record player was replaced by an eight-track player, then a cassette player, then a CD player, and most recently an mp3 player. Each offered distinct advantages over the other. In the same way spiritual technology is evolving and we are being called to raise our vibration faster than ever before.

Mid-Consciousness represents a vital step in this evolution. It allows us to be in a higher vibration all the time, not just when we sit and meditate. Several things come to play in this evolution process. First, technology has become easy for the masses. With this information has exploded. We now have the ability to not only get information but to be able to process more on a daily basis. We now think faster and in a more streamlined format. Mid-Consciousness is an example of this. Using your mind to achieve an altered state is a simple process. The symbol or icon that you use transports you to worlds beyond, or to any state that you desire.

Second, the world is also changing. In every evolution process there are milestones in which there is a significant change. We have arrived at this point and now reside in a more evolved energy. This also helps us to be able to have the luxury of spending more of our time and resources in the comfort of meeting our personal goals and dreams. This propels us into a time were we no longer spend most of our day in survival mode and are able to have time to explore our own interest. Mid-Consciousness will help carry you to develop those dreams and interests by letting you integrate the information you gather. As you develop skill in using Mid-Consciousness, you will use it not only to keep yourself in a better mental state, but you will also be able to assimilate your life interests at a deeper level.

Finally, in this time of new awakenings, humans are able to drop hard and fast mindsets that have imprisoned them in past times. As a society we no longer believe that any one person or organization is or has the ultimate truth. Therefore we are more apt to challenge research and question those that we allowed to hold power over us in the past.

This has launched us into an era of taking on the responsibility of taking care of ourselves. With this awakening we are freer to choose to use a new technology like Mid-Consciousness. As we continue to evolve, many will find that they no longer have to stay in "the Box". Developing our brains will become a natural way of life. We will enter a holistic lifestyle where mind, body and spirit are cared for in a unified manner.

In Exercise Five on page 79, you explored moving your body. In this chapter we combine movement and meditation into a powerful experience. What if it was not only possible to stay in state with your eyes open, but to use movement to deepen your intended state? The amazing news is that it is now possible to do just that. It's all about setting the intention and being connected to the body.

In Exercise Six you took the first baby steps into introducing movement into meditation when you:

- You used the movement of your hand tapping your forehead to initiate the process.

- You gently opened your eyes with the intention to remain in state.

In the previous chapter we explored the state of Divine Bliss. We recommend sticking with that intention in this exercise the first time you do it as you will be able to more accurately discern what is added by using movement.

When I (Janá) first began doing this I found the perfect

time and place. I had been experimenting with Mid-Consciousness at night. I loved the sensation of leaving to go on a trip to a higher dimension. But better yet was the feelings of coming back from dream time just as my senses begin to awaken. The first feeling of the sheets, the first light, the first sounds where so rich. My first thoughts were of Mid-Consciousness and my symbol. My symbol was of a portal spiraling back to earth. Then, I prolonged this time of wakening and drifting to sleep by slowly moving my body in soft and subtle ways. This worked so well that I begin the day coming out of dream time in my cocoon state and working the movements to larger and larger muscles. Stretching and rolling seem to be my favorites. I have also realized that the stiffness that I usually have is a lot better.

We hope you later repeat this exercise with other intended states such as peace, joy, relaxation or happiness and incorporate it into your daily life. Our lives have been greatly enhanced by using it and we would love to hear how your life was enhanced as well. Send us a link to your video or email your results (and photo if you have one) to results@htfgn.com.

Exercise Seven
Moving In Mid-Consciousness

This exercise builds on the Mid-Consciousness Basic Exercise by adding movement at the end. The other difference is that rather than waiting for your state to stabilize after step five, you are invited to do step six while your state is still deepening.

As you do step one below, record your state in your journal will help you track the changes that occur. Remember to assign a level, either one to ten or a percentage for each component of your state and to turn the page so that you won't see your old state when you complete the exercise.

1. **Assess Your State** – Notice how you are feeling without trying to change it or making yourself wrong for feeling that way. Record this in your journal so you can validate the changes that you experience.

2. **Intend Your State** – Set the intention to be in Divine Bliss or whatever other state you desire

3. **Automate Your Initial State** – Let go of how you are feeling and allow it to take care of itself

4. **Overlay the Symbol for Your Intended State** – Relax and let the symbol do the work for you.

5. **Push Start** – Tap your forehead and allow yourself to transform into your intended state.

6. **Intend to Deepen Your State** – Set the intention that opening your eyes will allow you to deepen into your intended state. Then gently open your eyes but keeping your attention and state inward and deepening. Allow whatever you see to deepen your state.

7. **Blink to Deepen Your State** – Intend that each time you blink your eyes, you deepen further into your desired state. Try deliberately blinking your eyes a few times. Each time you blink notice how your state deepens.

8. **Look Around** – Deliberately look around. Move your eyes from one object to the next. Each time allow the new image to stimulate and deepen your desired state. If you are doing this with other people it is fun to look at each other and see their state reflecting back the Divine Bliss that you are feeling.

Tip: If you are reading this exercise, allow each word you read to deepen your state.

9. **Pump Up Your State** – Take your hand and open and close it as if you were pumping up a blood pressure cuff. Intend that each time you do this your state deepens as if you could deepen your state easily and effortlessly by closing your hand.

10. **More Movement** – Introduce additional movements one at a time. Intend that each movement bring you deeper into your intended state. Starting with small movements, like tapping your foot on the ground and working your way up to larger movements like standing up or taking a step generally works best.

Tip: If you get distracted and lose your desired state or feel your movements are not deepening your state don't try to force it, instead go back to step one and continue in ease.

For optimal results repeat all ten steps at least three times. When you are done intend that each word you write in your journal deepens your state. Now, write about your experience, and record your state in your journal. Can you deepen your state while writing?

Chapter Eight
Pairing

Some experts think that the purpose of meditation is to listen to God. Others think it is for experiencing states of higher consciousness. In Buddhism one of the goals of meditation is to cultivate positive feelings like love and compassion. We believe that the goal of meditation is to allow you to experience the brightest, happiest, most fulfilling and most amazing life possible. This is a byproduct of being in the highest state of consciousness possible in each and every moment. The goal of Mid-Consciousness is exactly that: for you to be in the highest state of consciousness possible in each moment. This does not mean blissed out and withdrawn, but tuned in, engaged and dancing to the beat of your higher self (the most authentic, best possible version of you).

An old Zen quote says "You should sit in meditation for twenty minutes a day, unless you're too busy. Then you should sit for an hour." There is most certainly wisdom in this and we recommend making the time to meditate because even as little as twenty minutes of meditation a day can provide great benefits. Now imagine how quickly and dramatically your life could change for the better if you spent hours a day meditating. "There's just not enough time for that!", you may exclaim.

"What if it did not take any additional time?" we ask.

If you were given a magic remote control that allowed you to stop time for five minutes once each day, what would it be worth?

Would you sell it on eBay for $100 or would it be your dearest possession?

Imagine at the push of the button you could freeze everything except your thoughts, allowing you extra time in your day to change your state or experience higher states of consciousness. For us the magic remote would be a priceless treasure.

Pairing in Mid-Consciousness is even more valuable than the magic remote described above because it allows you to multitask. Each hour of the day can be used to experience higher states of consciousness, or any state you desire, while going about your day as before. Almost any activity that you do such as walking, typing, running, or even showering can be paired with a higher consciousness state.

In Exercise Seven p. 97, you learned to incorporate movement into meditation by using simple movements to bring you more into your desired state. In this chapter you will take it a step further and connect specific movements to desired states. We call this Pairing since it allows virtually any activity to be connected to a higher state of consciousness (or any desired state).

- Do you dread your boring or repetitive job?

- Is there a chore such as folding the laundry that you hate doing?

- What if each repetitive movement could be paired with a higher state of consciousness?

- Imagine how that can change things.

One afternoon I (Hale) discovered myself with a sink full of dirty, slimy, and smelly dishes. I really don't enjoy doing the dishes normally, but when they get stinky I really despise it. My kids were coming over and I was completely out of plates and bowls. I considered taking them out to dinner and avoiding the dishes a little longer, but decided to clean up the sink. Being a student of Mid-Consciousness I decided to experiment with pairing and set the intention that each time I picked up an item (plate, fork, etc.), rinse it off and put it in the dish washer; I would experience more Divine Bliss. By the time the sink was empty I was feeling great, truly spectacular and I even remember part of me wishing there were more slimy dishes in the sink.

This was in sharp contrast to the way I normally felt

about dirty dishes. It would have been easy for me to think "ick" every time I picked up a dish. I could have played the pity card: "Woe is me I can't afford a housekeeper." I could have played the blame game with myself: "Why didn't you rinse off and put each dish in the dishwasher as you used them. Then they would not of gotten icky." Instead I decided to use Mid-Consciousness and play the Divine Bliss game and I am glad that I did. Otherwise I would probably of been in a foul mood when the kids arrived and I certainly would not of remembered the experience of loading the dish washer over two years ago.

With pairing everything you do can bring you a connection to higher consciousness.

What if you just gave yourself a taste of it a few times a day? When eating take your first bite and think how absolutely divine each bite is.

Imagine thinking about the most wonderful trip you have taken when you are stuck at a traffic light or sitting in heavy traffic. Would that reduce your stress level?

What if your day consisted of 100 pit stops of divine feeling?

Wouldn't that be a big improvement?

We invite you to pair as many activities as you can throughout your day. Allow tasting the first bite of each meal to bring you more peace. Pair each step you take to increase joyfulness. The possibilities are endless. You can now do something wonderful with boring activities.

Each and every work task can be paired with and exciting new way to move and each movement can be paired with an intended state. Now, you can spend all day moving into the next fun activity and feeling terrific. Eventually, as the pairing pathways in your brain grow strong, you will automatically shift into feeling great without having to consciously initiate the process. You will have reprogrammed yourself to feel great all the time.

Exercise Eight
Basic Pairing

The Pairing exercise teaches you how to program a movement so that it deepens you into a specific state. In Exercise Seven you learned to incorporate movement into meditation. The Pairing exercise teaches you how to use movement to induce higher states of consciousness or any desired state. The first time you perform this exercise we invite you to again choose the state of Diving Bliss.

The movement can be anything from tapping your hand or taking a step to something more complicated like loading a dish in the dishwasher. Once paired the action can induce the preprogrammed state without having to go through the Mid-Consciousness process.

As you do step one below, record your state in your journal then close your eyes and continue the process. Whenever you open your eyes to read the next step allow the opening of your eyes and the reading of each word to honor and support you in reaching your intended state. Let's Begin:

1. **Assess Your State.**

2. **Set Your Intended State**

3. **Automate Your Initial State**

4. **Overlay the Symbol for Your Intended State** - Allow yourself to begin gravitating toward your intended state.

5. **Set Your Pairing Intention** - Set the intention that performing the movement will deepen you into your desired state.

6. **Push Start** – Tap your forehead and allow yourself to transform into your intended state.

7. **Inflate Your State** - Repeat the following steps until your intended state has reached the desired intensity or your state is no longer deepening with each movement.

   a. Perform the movement and feel your state deepening as you move.

   b. Assess your state.

8. **Persist the Pairing** - Now set the intention that whenever you perform the movement you will gravitate toward your intended state. Declare the process complete.

9. **Test the Pairing** – Allow your eyes to open and perform the movement. Do you notice a change in your state? Set an alarm to alert you in an hour. When

the alarm goes off perform the movement a few times and notice the change in your state.

You may have to repeat the process a few times for the pairing to take hold. Remember each time you do the steps above your rabbit path (p. 48) is growing bigger: the neural connections in your brain are growing stronger and your mind will find it easier and easier to choose the new path. Pretty soon all it will take to engage the new path is recalling the pairing intention and making the movement. After enough repetition the path will become a trench and any time you want to shift toward the programmed state, all you have to do is make the movement.

Chapter Nine
Neural Plasticity

Your brain works on electricity, much like how the lights in your house are wired. When you make new connections there are more ways to make light therefore you are illuminated in this way. You can reach a state where your mind is illuminated all of the time.

Sometimes there are problems that make you have outages in your brain just like sometimes the power is out in your home. Just like real power outages may only affect a few homes or could knock out a whole city, these outages in your brain can range from small to large depending on how much of your brain is affected. Very low-level situations in your life can cause you to go back into fear, which is darkness and create an outage. For example, anger is like a light bulb exploding in your mind, which leaves behind a hole of darkness. Note that darkness does not refer to evil, but simply indicates absence of light.

When you experience fear, anger or any other strong emotion it can trigger primitive areas of your brain. These areas of the brain do not have the capacity for higher thought and are not under conscious control. This is how people can freeze when frightened and temporarily become incapable of movement. Your thoughts become restricted like a wagon that only fits on rails of a certain width, it is difficult to jump off the track into a more positive thought or even to be aware of what is happening to you.

Imagine that someone says something that makes you furious. Your mind becomes like a runaway truck, dropping quickly into 2nd consciousness. You react automatically to what is happing and may say things you later regret. Just like a truck driver without breaks, you can't stop the stream of negative thoughts. However, you still can steer. All you need to safely recover is some level or uphill terrain. Unfortunately, you may not get this cooling off period. When you are angry with another person, they are most likely in their trenches as well, unable to rise out of them just as you are. So the argument escalates. This explains why normal people can become temporarily "crazy" and behaviors such as road rage happen. Afterwards, when the outage is repaired and mind starts function normally again, people often say things like "I had no idea what came over me!"

In Chapter Three, (p. 47) we discussed how these thought trenches were built in your mind and how to create new ones. In the exercise at the end of this chapter, you will learn how to reprogram a trigger so that an alternate pathway is created in your brain. This new pathway, though small, is capable of lifting your wagon of thought out of the deep trench. It's kind of like a runaway truck ramp for your thoughts so that in the heat of an argument, or even before it begins, you can suddenly jump into 3rd Consciousness and have the ability to choose a reasonable action.

One evening, I (Hale) watched the Adam Sandler movie "Big Daddy" with my kids. Unfortunately, soon after, one of them figured out how to let his spit hang down from his mouth and suck it in just like in the movie. Rather than appreciating his talent, I found this revolting and totally disgusting and told him not to do it. Over the next month I coaxed, and yelled at him, but he continued to do it. I noticed myself instantly becoming furious whenever he did the spit trick. About a week later, at one of my live events, I asked the participants to pick one thing that drove them crazy that they would like to change their response to. I instantly knew what I would work on so as I guided everyone through the exercise, I also participated.

The very next time my son did the spit trick, I felt my blood start to boil, but then, less than a second later, before I had time to say or do anything, I felt myself relax. Instead of thinking "He's doing that again just to make me mad" and being furious about it, I remember thinking "Oh, he's just doing that" and being neutral. This was an amazing shift and I was puzzled by it. I remember walking away thinking "Why did that bother me so much before?" and not being able to come up with a good answer. My son did the trick two or three more times over the next few weeks and I never again reacted to it, so he just quit doing it. The thing that I find most amazing is that my attempts to control his behavior failed and even made the situation worse. While my being OK with it allowed it to fade away, it certainly lends credibility to the quote "What you resist, persists" from the Swiss psychologist C.G. Jung.

With Mid-Consciousness we give you the tools to keep the electricity on all the time. Your brain does not have to have outages anymore. Imagine being able to work on these 3rd dimensional problems without having to turn the lights off or even dim them to where you are feeling poorly. With practice, the neurotransmitters in your mind become used to, and are plugged into Mid-Consciousness for long periods of time. This allows you to be in higher consciousness for increasingly longer periods which will naturally decrease the amount of time you spend feeling stressed or experiencing other undesirable states of being.

Through pairing you put your mind in Mid-Consciousness at different markers during the day. Each time you perform paired movements you naturally gravitate into an Intended State. That way you keep yourself up, in the higher states of consciousness, and feeling great. As this proceeds it is harder to go down. As you look at your mind in this state of light, alive with freely flowing electrical energy, you see it hardly ever flickers. There are no power source problems and even the worst problems of your day are viewed as a challenge, something you can change and bring up to your standard of light and love, instead of a problem that is difficult to face.

In this 3rd dimensional existence, practice is necessary. The light does not turn on by itself because you yourself are the light bulb. Staying plugged into source through Mid-Consciousness allows a steady stream of energy to flow to you to power your light. You don't have to work and toil to shine your light. However, you cannot indulge in low level issues and expect to live in bliss. Therefore we invite you to frame each situation and bring it into your mindset of light and love.

Yes, your relative or your friend is having a bad problem or even you. Until you are able to bring that into the love and light that Source has given you, you remain down in the dread, hatred and feelings of negativity. When you are ready you can surrender it to Source for the highest good. It is a letting go, but a letting go of elevating these things.

As with anything, it takes practice, not once a week like going to a meeting, but once a moment as you breathe. This may seem impossible, but there is a loophole. All of the practice does not have to be conscious. Pairing allows us to automate much of the practice. In order to understand this better we will use an example.

Imagine you had a light bulb in a remote location that you wanted to power. You could attach a small generator to a bicycle wheel and power the light whenever you pedaled. Unfortunately, as soon as the wheel stops spinning the light will go out. It would require a large amount of effort to keep the light lit. This is the problem with traditional meditation, for most people, as soon as they stop meditating, the wheel slows to a stop and they are back in their normal state of consciousness.

Now imagine that there is a stream nearby and you can connect the bicycle wheel to a water wheel so that as long as the water flows, the bicycle wheel will spin and the bulb will light. This is the way Pairing works. It takes some setup (going through the Pairing Exercise) but once it is working it will continue to power your desired state.

From time to time, you will still need to do maintenance, just like the water wheel could break, or need to be adjusted based on the flow of water, it may be necessary to adjust or strengthen your pairing.

To keep your light on all the time, try the following pairing:

116

Pair breathing in with bringing in the light and love that Source has given you.

Pair exhaling with taking out the things that you don't want.

This pairing will prompt you again and again each day to put your mind in higher consciousness. As this becomes your new norm, you will revert to higher thoughts instead of to the problems that are present.

We also encourage you to meet these problems in life in a straightforward manner. With you as higher consciousness you have no fear; therefore people do not hold your power; therefore you do not feel threatened. Most cases of problems are worried about far too much and when you get there the fear has penetrated your body, mind and soul and you have already given away your power to the other person or situation. It may seem like they have stolen your power, but in reality you gave it to them by engaging in worry and fear. When fear grips you it blocks the light. However the light does not stay still, if you don't want your strength, courage or power, you will reflect it. It is always an illusion that another has your power. What is true is that you are like a mirror, reflecting your power to them. The light is always shining on you, so as soon as you decide to take it in, it is yours. The other person has absolutely no say about that.

With higher consciousness you know that no one has power over you. They cannot hurt you. They cannot make you feel bad. So making a choice in this higher consciousness is very easy. With ease you say "I prefer that you do it this way" they have opportunity to negotiate with you but since you are in your power you are not intimidated. The power is equal and you can meet the situation head and allow it to resolve for the highest good of all concerned. This comes only after you have trained your mind to be in that place without faltering. It is the best and highest good for you and it is the best place for you to reside.

Yes, it is a challenge.

Yes, it will take time.

Yes, it is worth it.

Exercise Nine
Reprogramming A Trigger

This is another adaptation of the Mid Consciousness exercise. In Exercise Eight you paired an intended state with a physical movement. In this exercise you will program yourself to respond differently to a situation that has triggered you in the past by pairing the triggered state with your desired state.

1. **Identify the Trigger** - Pick a situation or circumstance that has frequently caused you to be triggered in the past. It could be related to a specific person or something more general like being stuck in traffic. Journal about your trigger.

2. **Pick an Intended State** - If you feel frustrated in traffic you might instead like to feel calm or peaceful. You could pick Divine Bliss, however be aware that you might unconsciously find yourself attracting pockets of traffic so that you can experience more Divine Bliss. For this reason I recommend picking a more neutral state such as feeling calm. Record you intended state in your journal.

3. **Assess Your State**

4. **Set Your Intended State (triggered)** – This time, your intended state is the triggered state. This is kind of like the bonus exercise Exploring "Negative" Emotions on page 55.

5. **Overlay the Symbol for Your Intended State** - Allow yourself to be in the intended state and allow the symbol to connect you more deeply with your intended state.

6. **Fill Yourself in With Light and Love** - Fill yourself in with light and love as you experience your triggered state. Don't use the love and light to push out your triggered state. Instead allow the light and love to change the way you relate to your triggered state so that you can relate to it in a loving manner. Remember to also treat yourself lovingly as you experience yourself in this triggered state.

7. **Fill the Situation in With Light and Love** – Visualize the person or situation that triggered being filled in with light and love.

8. **Set Your Intended State (desired)** - Decide how you would like to feel when you are triggered. Now set your intended state to the state you desire to be in.

9. **Automate Your Previous State** - Simply let it take care of itself.

120

10. **Overlay the Symbol of Your Desired State.**

11. **Push Start** – Tap once on your forehead with the intention to start the process of transforming into your intended state.

12. **Feel Your New State** - Keep your focus on the new state. See the symbol for your new state. Breathe in your new state.

13. **Pull up the Trigger** - While being in your new state, bring up the situation that triggered you. Do not put any attention on the old state. Continue feeling and experiencing your desired state as you allow the situation that triggered you to pass before you as if you were watching a movie of it.

14. **Dissolve the Trigger** - Allow the trigger to fade away and be fully in your desired state.

15. **Integrate Movement** - With your eyes still closed move your hands and arms and feel being in your desired state. Allow this new state to move and be dynamic.

16. **Become Present** - Allow your eyes to open and become fully present while still staying in your desired state.

17. **Complete the Process** - Bring the process to completion in a way that leaves you in your desired state.

18. **Record Your Experience** - Journal about your experience.

Save a page or two in your journal to record your experience the next time you are triggered. Some people experience dramatic shifts in how they feel and how they react the very next time they are triggered. If your shift is less than amazing, repeat the exercise again with the same trigger. Each time you repeat the exercise it strengthens and enlarges your runaway truck ramp, so it gets easier and easier to get to a place where you can respond in a manner you desire instead of reacting when triggered. Eventually your new neural pathways will be so strong that you naturally bypass the trigger. Once this happens, your default response to the triggering situation will be the one you have programmed instead of the old behavior and this will be your new "normal" state of being.

Chapter Ten
Conclusion

Your mind has expanded since you began reading this book and doing the exercises. The whole point of Mid-Consciousness is to grow your mind so that you can stay in a state that is not negatively affected by your 3rd dimensional world. This does not mean tuned out or disengaged. It means to be fully present in the moment, alive and engaged, yet non-attached. You are the master of your state. What someone says to you may cause you emotional pain and you may feel the momentary pull toward anger, anxiety or sadness. That's living in the real world, but you don't have to stay there. With Mid Consciousness you can acknowledge your state and then relax back into your desired state.

You can even do this aloud "When you said _____ to me I felt _____." This raises awareness, allows the conversation to deepen, and promotes an environment where healing to occur. Often, when dealing with less aware individuals, the response is something like "Well I said that because you ..." If you can hold in the loving and not get triggered by such blame statements then you can respond lovingly and eventually a breakthrough can occur.

If, however, you drop down to a lower level of consciousness and begin defending yourself against the accusations the situation may resolve itself badly. Even if you win an emotional argument, you may walk away with battle scars and get triggered more quickly next time.

Bringing awareness to what is happening can often raise realm of consciousness the other person is operating from. During a break at a couples workshop, Dr. Ron Hulnick and I (Hale) were discussing pairing and consciousness. I remember him saying something like "The one with the highest consciousness has the most responsibility." I totally agree and consider this added responsibility a gift, not a burden.

By raising your consciousness you can take a greater role in the evolution of this planet. Every disagreement that ends with compassion and a deeper understanding of each other brings us closer together, and every hateful thing that you do not say because you are able to respond instead of reacting makes the world a better place. This does not mean saying nothing, stuffing the feeling, and walking away annoyed. Instead tune in to the authentic you, your highest self and express from there. It is sometimes in ones highest good to hear harsh words and sometimes even to say them. However, before erupting in string of expletives, we invite you to consider whether they are for the benefit of the other person, or the benefit of your ego.

I (Hale) have a deep desire to affect positive and lasting change in this world. While this book sprang from that desire, I would not have been able to write it without first growing and evolving myself. Ironically, now that the book is complete, believe that what is most important is how I am being in each and every moment instead of improving the lives of others. So ultimately what Janá and I have written is the guidebook that I needed most. We lovingly hope you find it useful as well.

Review & Checklist

As a result of reading this book and doing the exercises you now have many new capabilities. Review the checklist below and see which techniques you have mastered and put into practice. The exercise and page number where the technique was taught is listed after each technique.

- ✓ Are you able to bring yourself Present at will? Exercise One, p. 25

- ✓ Do you understand the realms of consciousness and know which realm you are operating from? The Realms of Consciousness, p. 33

- ✓ Can you Ground yourself and stay Grounded throughout your day? Grounding, p. 43

✓ Are you aware of your State? Can you turn it up or down at will? Exploring "Negative" Emotions, p. 53

✓ Can you take yourself through Mid-Consciousness and arrive in Divine Bliss without having to refer back to the exercise? Exercise Six, p. 89

✓ Can you use physical movement to break yourself free from a crystallized emotional state? Exercise Five, p. 55

✓ Can you use movement to deepen into your intended state? Exercise Seven, p. 97

✓ Have you Paired each section of your day with an intended state of consciousness such that you have at multiple touch points with higher consciousness each day? Exercise Eight, p. 107

✓ When a new situation triggers you, can you put a stop to it by reprogramming the trigger? Reprogramming A Trigger, p. 119

How did you do? As humans we love to keep score. If you feel like you did well then keeping score on this assessment worked for you. If you feel like you haven't mastered any the techniques don't beat yourself up. The truth is that after practicing these techniques for over two years I (Hale) have not mastered any of them. I continue to have new awareness' and new experiences as I practice the techniques. This simply means I am growing. I choose not to judge myself or beat myself up over my lack of progress and I invite you to do the same.

We hope you put into practice what you have learned. We want you to become more and more comfortable being in higher consciousness. There are so many layers of magnificence for us to show you as you are able to create your heaven, your own paradise, your own Garden of Eden right here, living in this 3rd dimensional existence on this little blue planet we call earth. We sincerely wish this for you.

Finally give yourself a big pat on the back for completing this book. We see through your human appearance to the awesome, magnificent, and glorious being of light and love that you truly are.

For additional support, make sure you join our exclusive mailing list for book readers here:

www.htfgn.com/readertools

Love & Light,

Hale & Janá

68442171R00080

Made in the USA
San Bernardino, CA
03 February 2018